The Princess
and the Pea

Collect all the books in the
Magical Princess *series*

The Princess and the Pea

Written and illustrated by

Sally Gardner

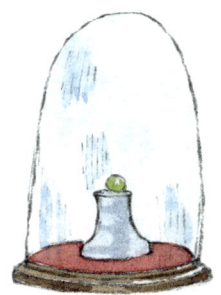

Orion
Children's Books

The Princess and the Pea first appeared in *A Book of Princesses*
first published in Great Britain in 1997
by Orion Children's Books
This edition first published in Great Britain in 2011
by Orion Children's Books
a division of the Orion Publishing Group Ltd
Orion House
5 Upper St Martin's Lane
London WC2H 9EA
An Hachette UK Company

3 5 7 9 10 8 6 4

A catalogue record for this book is available from the British Library.

ISBN 978 1 4440 0245 4

Printed in China

The Orion Publishing Group's policy is to use papers that are natural,
renewable and recyclable products made from wood grown in sustainable forests.
The logging and manufacturing processes are expected to conform
to the environmental regulations of the country of origin.

www.orionbooks.co.uk

For Katharine Barrington,
with all my love

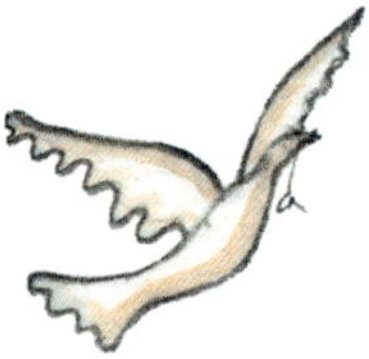

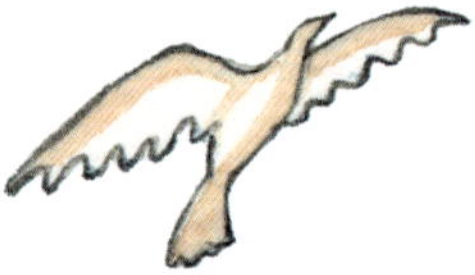

 # Contents

 # Chapter One

Once upon a time there lived
a prince who wished very much to
marry a real princess.

His search for a bride took him
around the world and back again.

That is a very long way indeed.

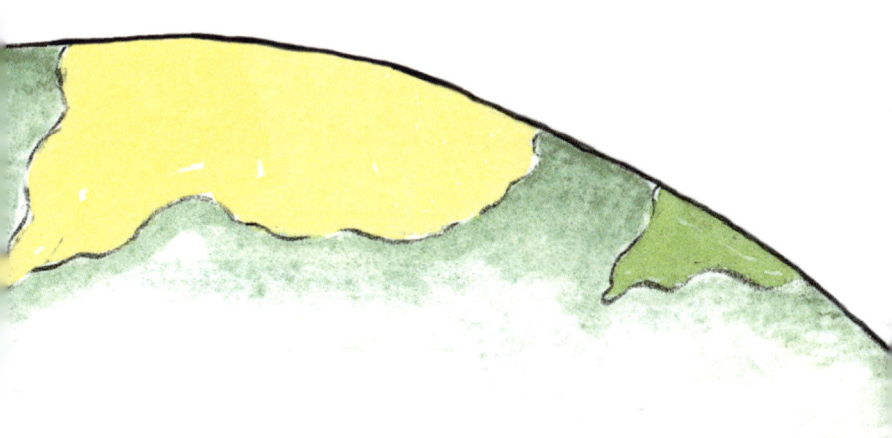

He met lots of girls who called
themselves princesses:

pretty ones,

plain ones,

happy ones,

sad ones and
mad ones.

But there was always something
not quite right.

It was a problem. How was he to know if they were real princesses? At last he gave up and went home, feeling very upset.

The king and queen agreed
with their son. There was no point
in marrying a girl who was not
a real princess.

What was to be done?

 # Chapter Two

Then, one wild and stormy night,
a princess was being driven home
from a party.

The princess's car went too fast
round a corner and she was
thrown into a ditch.

The driver did not see what
had happened and carried on,
leaving the princess all alone.

"Well, this is a pickle,"
said the princess,
picking herself up.
"I'd better try and find
some shelter."

She walked through the
howling wind and pouring rain
until she came to a palace.

"There must be someone here who can help me," the princess said to herself.

 # Chapter Three

The princess rang the bell and was brought before the king and queen.

She looked a terrible mess.

Her hair was dripping wet,
her dress was torn, her shoes were all
muddy, and she had
lost her crown.

The king and queen were
surprised that this girl called
herself a princess, but they
were kind enough to invite
her to stay.

She could not very
well go out again on
a night like this.

The princess had a bath and was
given some clean clothes.

Then she was brought to
the great hall for supper.

The prince thought she looked very nice,
but what was the point of falling
in love when she might not
be a real princess at all?

The queen had an idea.

"Too many girls these days," she said, "pretend to be princesses. There is only one way of knowing for certain if this is a real princess."

Chapter Four

The queen went into the girl's bedroom and placed one tiny pea under the mattress.

Then she ordered twenty more
mattresses to be put on top.

She was still not sure if there were enough mattresses, so she ordered another twenty to be put on top of them.

When the princess went to bed
she needed a ladder to climb to
the top of all those mattresses.
But she was a guest, so she
couldn't very well ask why there
were so many when just one
would have done nicely.

41

The bed, for all its forty-one
mattresses, was very
uncomfortable.

The princess was sure the mattresses
were filled with rocks instead
of feathers.

 # Chapter Five

In the morning the king and queen
asked the princess how she had slept.

"I couldn't sleep at all, your majesty,"
said the princess.

"The bed was so lumpy and bumpy that
I am bruised black and blue all over."

The king and queen were delighted.

There could
be no doubt
that this was a

real
princess.

Only a real princess is tender
enough to feel one tiny pea
through so many mattresses.

Chapter Six

The prince was keen to
marry the princess.

The princess was happy to marry him too, for it is not easy to find a real prince these days.

Real princes

are

quite rare.

In no time at all they were
married, and they lived
happily ever after.

Now, isn't that
a tender-hearted tale?

As for the pea, it was put in
a museum, or was it the soup?

Do you know? I quite forget.

Look out for

Cinderella

Sleeping
Beauty

The Frog Prince

Snow White